JUGGLING CHAINSAWS ON A TIGHTROPE

REALLIFE**STUFF**FOR**MEN** ON STRESS

A BIBLE DISCUSSION GUIDE FEATURING

NAVPRESS®

BRINGING TRUTH TO LIFE

OUR GUARANTEE TO YOU

We believe so strongly in the message of our books that we are making this quality guarantee to you. If for any reason you are disappointed with the content of this book, return the title page to us with your name and address and we will refund to you the list price of the book. To help us serve you better, please briefly describe why you were disappointed. Mail your refund request to: NavPress, P.O. Box 35002, Colorado Springs, CO 80935.

The Navigators is an international Christian organization. Our mission is to reach, disciple, and equip people to know Christ and to make Him known through successive generations. We envision multitudes of diverse people in the United States and every other nation who have a passionate love for Christ, live a lifestyle of sharing Christ's love, and multiply spiritual laborers among those without Christ.

NavPress is the publishing ministry of The Navigators. NavPress publications help believers learn biblical truth and apply what they learn to their lives and ministries. Our mission is to stimulate spiritual formation among our readers.

ISBN 1-57683-819-6

Cover design by Arvid Wallen
Cover illustration by Jared Lee
Creative Team: Steve Parolini, Cara Iverson, Pat Reinheimer

Written and compiled by Tim McLaughlin

Some of the anecdotal illustrations in this book are true to life and are included with the permission of the persons involved. All other illustrations are composites of real situations, and any resemblance to people living or dead is coincidental.

Printed in Canada

1 2 3 4 5 6 7 8 9 10 / 09 08 07 06 05

FOR A FREE CATALOG OF NAVPRESS BOOKS & BIBLE STUDIES,
CALL 1-800-366-7788 (USA) OR 1-800-839-4769 (CANADA)

CONTENTS

ABOUT THE
REALLIFESTUFFFORMEN
SERIES

Let your love dictate how you deal with me;
  teach me from your textbook on life.
I'm your servant — help me understand what that means,
  the inner meaning of your instructions. . . .
Break open your words, let the light shine out,
  let ordinary people see the meaning.

—Psalm 119:124-125,130

We're all yearning for understanding—for truth, wisdom, and hope. Whether we suffer in the simmering quiet of uncertainty or the megaphone cacophony of disbelief, we long for a better life—a more meaningful existence. We want to be Men Who Matter. But the fog of "real life stuff" we encounter every day obscures the life we crave, so we go on with the way things are.

Sometimes we pretend we don't care.

We do.

Sometimes we pretend everything is fine.

It isn't.

The truth is, the real life stuff matters. In that fog, there are things about our wives, our children, our friends, our work, and, most significantly, ourselves that cause varying degrees of distress, discomfort, and dis-ease.

The Real Life Stuff for Men series is a safe place for exploring the truth about that fog. But it's not a typical Bible study. You won't find any fill-in-the-blank questions in these pages. Nor will you find any pat answers. It's likely you'll come away with more questions rather than fewer. But through personal reflection and—in a small group—lively discussion (the best part of a Bible study anyway), these books will take you where you *need* to go and bring greater hope and meaning to your life.

Each of the books in this series provides a place to ask the hard questions of yourself and others, a place to find comfort in the chaos, a place to enlarge understanding, and—with the guidance of the Holy Spirit—a place to discover Real Life Hope that brings meaning to the everyday.

INTRODUCTION

We're safe from the tigers now. But no one has told our Cro-Magnon brains the good news. We still react to stress the same way, but now our physiology works to hurt us, not help. Today the twig snap comes with an innocent "Can you drop by my office?" and the lion roars via e-mail. Yet our bodies still behave as they did 300 centuries ago, flooding our systems with adrenaline every time a threat looms—whether it's physical, emotional, or financial. And because we can no longer run for safety when stress attacks, our need for fight or flight is never addressed.

The maddening thing is that we're feeling all these symptoms not in the company of a ravenous predator, but rather in those lonely, wee small hours when we're awake and our partner's asleep and the bills on the kitchen table are laughing at us. And this is supposed to be nature's way of keeping us alive. Instead, it's killing us, just as surely as—perhaps even more surely than—the fat we ate for dinner or the genetic time bomb lurking in our DNA.

Stress demands action, and action is not what our orderly world is built for. Stress makes men do things they shouldn't do, because they have to do something. Stress puts a besotted, heartbroken husband behind the wheel of a car; lures a 17-year-old expectant dad into the middle of a drug bust; pushes an honest businessman across the threshold into racketeering; and makes us snap at our partners, or our kids, with words we can't take back, that start us down the path to all sorts of costly consequences.

—FROM "HISTORY OF STRESS," ON MENSHEALTH.COM

At work, you think of the children you have left at home. At home, you think of the work you've left unfinished. Such a struggle is unleashed within yourself. Your heart is rent.

—GOLDA MEIR

"I'm leaving you well and whole. That's my parting gift to you. Peace. I don't leave you the way you're used to being left—feeling abandoned, bereft. So don't be upset. Don't be distraught."

—JESUS, AS RECORDED IN JOHN 14:27

Once upon a time, towns were smaller, behavior was more predictable, options were fewer, and beliefs were less questioned. Sure, there were still money problems and family dilemmas and secret doubts. Yet when you read journals and newspapers and histories from the past and when you talk to the elderly, you get the feeling that life just flowed. It didn't bulldoze you, as it seems to today. Western culture has not always been this noisy, this invasive.

This *stressful.*

Christian men experience stress in their own peculiar vise. The surface screwing down, tightening on you is the world of your daily reality: an orthodontist's bill that was due last week, the impossibility of leaving a job where a passive-aggressive boss gives you migraines, a marriage you feel more resigned to than passionate about.

The vise's other face—the stationary, unmoving one against which you're squeezed—is often your faith. It's pretty darn solid, or feels like it. You've been told it is immovable, as good as granite. And it's been there—*he's* been there—when you most needed help, guidance, comfort, a firm foundation. Yet at other times, such reliability has turned to pain when you feel crushed between merciless reality and unyielding beliefs.

So what in heaven's name did Jesus have in mind when he promised us peace?

That's what we'll be exploring in *Juggling Chainsaws on a Tightrope.* Sound like a simple task? It's not. (Have you ever grabbed the wrong end of one of those chainsaws?) Faced with stress at home, at work, in our relationships, and in ourselves, what does our faith have to say that could possibly reduce any of it? Where is God in all of this? And what do our and others' experiences say to us about stress, about how to cope with it, about how to reduce it?

Jesus never had to deal with rush-hour traffic on the freeway, or with an adolescent child who thumbed her nose at his standards, or with a tedious job and a tyrannical boss. Jesus *did* experience overwhelming human demands on him, friends and followers who ended up thumbing their noses at him, and harassment by the authorities.

Maybe Jesus, and the Word that narrates his life, just might hold some hope for us as we try to identify and reduce our stress and, in the process, find a little corner of that peace Jesus promised us.

HOW TO USE THIS DISCUSSION GUIDE

This discussion guide is meant to be completed on your own and in a small group. So before you begin, line up a discussion group. Perhaps you already participate in a men's group. That works. Maybe you know a few friends who could do coffee once a week. That works, too. Ask around. You'll be surprised how many of your coworkers, team members, and neighbors would be interested in a small-group study—especially a study like this that doesn't require vast biblical knowledge. A group of four to six is optimal—any bigger and one or more members will likely be shut out of discussions. Your small group can also be two. Choose a friend who isn't afraid to "tell it like it is." Make sure each person has his own copy of the book.

1. *Read* the Scripture passages and other readings in each lesson on your own. Let it all soak in. Then use the white space provided to "think out loud on paper." Note content in the readings that troubles you, inspires you, confuses you, or challenges you. Be honest. Be bold. Don't shy away from the hard things. If you don't understand the passage, say so. If you don't agree, say that, too. You may choose to go over the material in one thirty- to forty-five-minute focused session. Or perhaps you'll spend twenty minutes a day on the readings.

2. *Think* about what you read. Think about what you wrote. Always ask, "What does this mean?" and "Why does this matter?" about

the readings. Compare different Bible translations. Respond to the questions we've provided. You may have a lot to say on one topic, little on another. That's okay. Come back to this when you're in your small group. Allow the experience of others to broaden your wisdom. You'll be stretched here—called upon to evaluate what you've discovered and asked to make practical sense of it. In community, that stretching can often be painful and sometimes even embarrassing. But your willingness to be transparent—your openness to the possibility of personal growth—will reap great rewards.

3. *Pray* as you go through the entire session: before you read a word, in the middle of your thinking process, when you get stuck on a concept or passage, and as you approach the time when you'll explore these passages and thoughts together in a small group. Pause when you need to ask God for inspiration or when you need to cry out in frustration. Speak your prayers, be silent, or use the prayer starter we've provided and write a prayer at the end of each lesson.

4. *Live.* (That's "live" as in "rhymes with give" as in "Give me something I can really use in my life.") Before you meet with your small group, complete as much of this section as you can (particularly the "What I Want to Discuss" section). Then, in your small group, ask the hard questions about what the lesson means to you. Dig deep for relevant, reachable goals. Record your real-world plan in the book. Commit to following through on these plans, and prepare to be held accountable.

5. *Follow up.* Don't let the life application drift away without action. Be accountable to small-group members and refer to previous "Live" as in "rhymes with give" sections often. Take time at the beginning of each new study to review. See how you're doing.

6. *Repeat* as necessary.

SMALL-GROUP STUDY TIPS

After going through each week's study on your own, it's time to sit down with others and go deeper. Here are a few thoughts on how to make the most of your small-group discussion time.

Set ground rules. You don't need many. Here are two:

First, you'll want group members to make a commitment to the entire eight-week study. A binding legal document with notarized signatures and commitments written in blood probably isn't necessary, but you know your friends best. Just remember this: Significant personal growth happens when group members spend enough time together to really get to know each other. Hit-and-miss attendance rarely allows this to occur.

Second, agree together that everyone's story is important. Time is a valuable commodity, so if you have an hour to spend together, do your best to give each person ample time to express concerns, pass along insights, and generally feel like a participating member of the group. Small-group discussions are not monologues. However, a one-person-dominated discussion isn't always a bad thing. Not only is your role in a small group to explore and expand your own understanding, it's also to support one another. If someone truly needs more of the floor, give it to him. There will be times when the needs of the one outweigh the needs of the many.

Use good judgment and allow extra space when needed. *Your* time might be next week.

Meet regularly. Choose a time and place, and stick to it. No one likes showing up to Coffee Cupboard at 6:00 AM, only to discover the meeting was moved to Breakfast Barn at seven. Consistency removes stress that could otherwise frustrate discussion and subsequent personal growth. It's only eight weeks. You can do this.

Talk openly. If you enter this study with shields up, you're probably not alone. And you're not a "bad person" for your hesitation to unpack your life in front of friends or strangers. Maybe you're skeptical about the value of revealing the deepest parts of who you are to others. Maybe you're simply too afraid of what might fall out of the suitcase. You don't have to go to a place where you're uncomfortable. If you want to sit and listen, offer a few thoughts, or even express a surface level of your own pain, go ahead. But don't neglect what brings you to this place—that longing for meaning. You can't ignore it away. Dip your feet in the water of brutally honest discussion, and you may choose to dive in. There is healing here.

Stay on task. Refrain from sharing material that falls into the "too much information" category. Don't spill unnecessary stuff, such as your wife's penchant for midnight bedroom belly dancing or your boss's obsession with Jennifer Aniston. This is about discovering how you can be a better person.

If structure isn't your group's strength, try a few minutes of general comments about the study, and then take each "Live" question one at a time and give everyone in the group a chance to respond. That should get you into the meat of matters pretty quickly.

Hold each other accountable. That "Live" section is an important gear in the growth machine. If you're really ready for positive change—for spiritual growth—you'll want to take this section seriously. Not only should you personally be thorough as you summarize your discoveries, practical as you compose your goals, and realistic as you determine the plan for accountability, you must hold everyone else in the group accountable for doing these things. Be lovingly, brutally honest as you examine each other's "Live" section. Don't hold back—this is where the rubber meets the road. A lack of openness here may send other group members skidding off that road.

I CAN'T KEEP UP WITH THE WORKLOAD

"I could be fired or downsized anytime. I know
I'm not the only one waking up at 4 a.m.
worrying about losing the house."

THE BEGINNING PLACE

It's often around summer vacation that you most feel the stress of a
workload. You schedule a vacation with your supervisor the previous
winter, and as the weeks wind down to your anticipated time off, you
work weekends and nights the last week or two just to be away from
your desk for two weeks. Sometimes you even delay your vacation a
day or two desperately tying up loose ends.

When you finally get to the lake (or resort or beach or campsite
or hotel), it takes three days just to wind down. And then the last few
days of vacation, your stress level starts rising again as you anticipate
returning to several hundred e-mails and voice mails—not to mention
more than a few fires to put out. The net result of your fourteen-day
vacation: about five good, relaxing days.

This is no longer our fathers' and grandfathers' world, where
a worker's loyalty to a company was rewarded by a secure career
followed by a lifelong pension. No one—CEO or driver, technician
or receptionist—is immune to being downsized out of a job. What
used to be a win-win covenant between employer and employee
has gone obscenely out of balance: The purchasing power of wages

has shriveled until it now takes two full-time incomes to sustain a small family. Health benefits, which have traditionally kept even disgruntled employees on the job, are similarly drying up fast. In short, corporations have typically abandoned whatever loyalty they may have had to their employees and invested that loyalty unmistakably and lucratively in their stockholders.

And we haven't even mentioned the daily stresses of your specific responsibilities and duties. As if they even matter with dispensability breathing down your neck all day, every day.

How do you manage to be productive with this kind of stress? How does your workplace stress influence the other aspects of your life—your primary relationships (marriage, family, close friendships), your leisure (or your attempt at it), your faith? Where do you find momentary release from such stress? Are you considering taking a deliberate step into a lot more or a lot less stress? Or are you the type that is actually energized when the occupational odds get high?

Use the space below to summarize your beginning place for this lesson. Describe your workplace realities, anxieties, and specific stress points. We'll start here and then go deeper.

READ A Churning Stomach

Job 30:27

> My stomach's in a constant churning, never settles down.
>> Each day confronts me with more suffering.

THINK

- To what degree do you identify with Job's lament here?
- When you have thoughts like this, do you tend to dismiss them as mere whining? Explain.
- What about your job's workload makes your stomach churn?
- Is this churning something you could relieve, or something to simply live with?

PRAY

God, show me how . . .

READ Always Saving the Day

From the *Youthworker* interview "Coping with Stress and Burnout in Youth Ministry" with Carmen Renee Berry[1]

The messiahs have no problems, no needs; they are the controllers of the bad people and the helpers of the good people.

This is a dangerous hook, because when you're feeling good and confident, you'll take on more than you should. But when you're feeling badly about yourself, you feel you're not worthy enough to take time for. "I can't cut back, [others] need me," you tell yourself. "So much is going on in church right now. I know I should take a couple of days off, but I have too much going on."

And it becomes an addictive lifestyle. To complicate matters, churches often reinforce it. For the most part, churches underpay and overwork their employees. A church staff member gets one day off, but is generally on call 24 hours a day. The idea of a six-day workweek is unheard of in most other professions, but not in churches. Even if you're giving residential treatment, you get two or three days off a week. Because the ministry has such an unrealistic demand and pays so poorly, it sets you up for stress with a double whammy. . . .

You wrap it up in Scripture and . . . [convey] the message that if you're a really good person, you're overachieving. Really good Christians are involved in every activity. Really good Christians are there whenever the church is open. Really good Christians do nothing for themselves, but are always involved in ministry programs. A [Christian leader] living in the addictive lifestyle of stress emphasizes in his or her teaching how to take care of other people while ignoring the signals God has given you about yourself.

THINK

- Are you a messiah? Are you inclined to think that if *you* don't do something, it won't get done?
- If your job is a ministry job, does this description sound familiar? To what degree does it reflect your experience?
- Even if your job isn't a ministry job, what if any similarities are there between this description and your experience?
- In what ways do you feel the trickle-down effect in your workplace of the boss's work ethic (and work hours, work style, and so on) to your office? Is it a healthy or unhealthy trickle?

PRAY

Lord, help me to see . . .

READ Fewer Places to Hide

From *A Minute of Margin*, by Richard A. Swenson, M.D.[2]

It goes without saying that most employers and managers are more invested in the job than the people they supervise. This often makes for a natural asymmetry between their expectations and those of their employees. Meanwhile workers, who might not be interested in 24/7 availability, have fewer places to hide. "Where were you yesterday?" the boss might ask. "I was trying to reach you all day!" Never mind that it was Saturday and you were camping with the children. Or that it was Christmas Day and you were halfway to Grandma's house. "You know your boss is on vacation," quipped one employee, "when you receive 3 percent fewer emails from her." . . .

Communication technology has entered a new era and continuous accessibility is now a real possibility. It is time for a rational discussion of the massive implications this holds for workplace sustainability, morale, productivity, efficiency, innovation, and creativity. It turns out, if you really want to be a good worker, there are times when you must be *disconnected* from the office.

THINK

- How does the availability afforded by e-mail and cell phones impact your stress on the job?
- In what ways does this 24/7 communication decrease stress on the job?
- What experiences have you had with 24/7 availability that have challenged your ability to separate work and nonwork time?
- What is the value in separating yourself from 24/7 availability? How can you do this?

THINK (CONTINUED)

PRAY

Lord, give me wisdom to . . .

READ Fueled

Romans 12:11

Don't burn out; keep yourselves fueled and aflame.

THINK

- Recall the last time you really felt fueled and aflame on your job. How long ago was it? How long did that season last? What caused it to end?
- Paul says, "Don't burn out"; your workload seems to require it. Where's middle ground? *Is* there middle ground?
- What are some things you do that keep you fueled?

PRAY

Lord, guide me . . .

READ Disguising Stress

From *Reducing Stress*, by Tim Hindle[3]

Take note of the predominant attitudes and behavior at work to assess your organization's approach to stress. If stress is an intrinsic part of a job, it is often easier to glamorize it than to change working practices. A case study of this:

The managing director of a large commercial company often boasted that he spent more time out of the office on business trips than at his desk.

When asked to develop a new product line, he worked day and night to coordinate the efforts of different departments. He flew around the world in search of information and contacts to ensure that the new line would be a success. His free time shrank, his home life suffered, he was constantly tired, and he ate poorly—but because he knew that his company was depending on him, he continued. He began to experience severe stomach pains and was diagnosed with a peptic ulcer.

This case reflects a common problem: many high-powered employees accept the heavy workload imposed by their companies and brag about their responsibilities to disguise stress and fears of failure.

In certain work cultures, some stress is unavoidable: oil and mining companies expect employees to spend time away from home, and management consulting firms and investment banks expect their staff to work long hours. It is important to be able to identify unacceptable levels of workplace stress; disguising stress can make it harder to deal with the long-term effects.

THINK

- What is the workplace culture like at your job? Do the higher-ups model—or perhaps even glamorize—a stressful work style?

- How is stress disguised at your workplace?
- What have you observed or experienced of this in ministry environments, where a stressful workplace culture is connected to spirituality?
- How successful or unsuccessful have you been in cultivating a reputation as an energetic and productive employee without stressing out yourself (and your family, friends, and so on)?

PRAY

Father, give me margin . . .

READ No Time to Waste

1 Corinthians 7:29-31

There is no time to waste, so don't complicate your lives unnecessarily. Keep it simple—in marriage, grief, joy, whatever. Even in ordinary things—your daily routines of shopping, and so on. Deal as sparingly as possible with the things the world thrusts on you. This world as you see it is on its way out.

THINK

- How likely is it that Paul would have included your workload in his "whatever" category? Explain.
- Is your job situation such that you can "keep it simple"? Why or why not?
- How do you reconcile the modern tendency to define yourself by your job with the apostle's suggestion to "deal as sparingly as possible with the things the world thrusts on you"?
- What's one thing you could do tomorrow to uncomplicate your workload?

PRAY

God, help me to simplify . . .

LIVE

What I Want to Discuss

What have you discovered this week that you definitely want to discuss with your small group? Write that here. Then begin your small-group discussion with these thoughts.

So What?

Use the following space to summarize the truths you uncovered about workplace and workload stress and what you really need to do to reduce that stress. Review your "Beginning Place" if you need to remember where you began. How does God's truth impact the "next step" in your journey?

Then What?

What is one practical thing you can do to apply what you've discovered? Describe how you would put this into practice. What steps would you take? Remember to think realistically—an admirable but unreachable goal is as good as no goal. Discuss your goal in your small group to further define it.

How?

Identify how you will be held accountable to the goal you described. Who will be on your support team? What are their responsibilities? How will you measure the success of your plan? Write the details here.

I DON'T MAKE ENOUGH MONEY

"May the Lord smite me with it. And may I never recover."—Tevye, in *Fiddler on the Roof*, in response to a friend's warning that money is the world's curse.

A REMINDER:

Before you dive into this study, spend a little time reviewing what you wrote in the previous lesson's "Live" sections. How are you doing? Check with your small-group members and review your progress toward the specified goals. If necessary, adjust your goals and plans, and then recommit to them.

THE BEGINNING PLACE

This is not just break-room bellyaching. The purchasing power of a paycheck has been sliding since the 1970s, and signs point to only more of the same. So in one sense, the typical American worker can indeed say, with justification, that he doesn't make enough money.

There are two obvious proofs of this. Proof number one: the unlikelihood that one income can support a middle-class household. A half century ago, a grown man could support a wife and children by selling shoes in a small Main Street shop—and still have money left to put aside for retirement. Now? Most retail shoe-store clerks are students willing to work for minimum wage.

Proof number two: the growing chasm between the salaries of top executives and the rank-and-file worker. Not many years ago, CEOs in Standard & Poor's 500 corporations made 209 times the average U.S.

factory worker's pay. It wasn't always like this: Most economists agree that the ratio began its steep ascent during the supply-and-demand years of the Reaganomic '80s. Before that, execs pulled down a paltry forty or fifty times what their assembly-line workers earned.

Entrepreneurs are lined up at your e-mail inbox, if not your door, to guarantee you a way across that income gap: "You can fulfill your earning potential! From home! Turn the skills you already have into cash! Unleash the power within you! Claim the wealth God has promised you!"

Meanwhile, income-triggered stress just piles up. Maybe an investment went south, leaving you wondering how you'll ever repay the loan you took out. Or maybe, just once, you'd like to shop for groceries without coupons and a calculator.

So how do you live with stress induced by money—or the lack of it? When in your past were you flush—or at least more at peace than you are now about not being flush? Where is God in all of this, anyway? You hear regularly that he wants you to have "enough"—but what exactly is "enough"? Why can't your "enough" resemble the "enough" of that business-owner elder at your church—the one with the summer home on the lake who takes his family on regular European vacations? Is it the blessing of God, luck in the stock market, or family connections he was born into? What does your own need for more money say about you, if anything?

Use the space below to summarize your beginning place for this lesson. Describe your financial realities, your financial stresses, and how you live with them (or don't). We'll start here and then go deeper.

READ Computing Financial Stress

From "The Social Readjustment Rating Scale," by Thomas H. Holmes and Richard H. Rahe[1]

What is your stress level? Look back at your last year and tally the points using the following chart.

Life Event	Point Value	Life Event	Point Value
Death of spouse	100	Change in responsibilities at work	29
Divorce	73	Son or daughter leaving home	29
Marital separation	65	Trouble with in-laws	29
Jail term	63	Outstanding personal achievement	28
Death of close family member	63	Spouse begins or stops work	26
Personal injury or illness	53	Begin or end school	26
Marriage	50	Change in living conditions	25
Fired at work	47	Revision of personal habits	24
Marital reconciliation	45	Trouble with boss	23
Retirement	45	Change in work hours or conditions	20
Change in health of family member	44	Change in residence	20
Pregnancy	40	Change in schools	20
Sex difficulties	39	Change in recreation	19
Gain of new family member	39	Change in church activities	19
Business readjustment	39	Change in social activities	18
Change in financial state	38	Mortgage or loan less than $10,000	17
Death of close friend	37	Change in sleeping habits	16
Change to different line of work	36	Change in number of family get-togethers	15
Change in number of arguments with spouse	35	Change in eating habits	15
Mortgage or loan over $10,000	31	Vacation	13
Foreclosure of mortgage or loan	30	Christmas	12
		Minor violations of the law	11

Holmes and Rahe found that people with scores over 300 points for one year had an 80 percent risk of becoming seriously ill or vulnerable to depression during the following year. Those with scores between 200 and 300 points still had an impressive 50 percent, or moderate, risk. Those with scores below 200 were at relatively low risk. Although these statistics cannot predict the risk for any particular individual, they do confirm the correlation between life-change stress and both physical and emotional health.

THINK

- So what's your score? Is it higher or lower than last year at this time?
- How many of the scale's forty-three life events are fundamentally financial or have direct financial manifestations? How many of the top dozen are?
- Are you anticipating any additional or different items in the coming year? Are they fundamentally financial?
- Did your score surprise you? More stress than you thought? Less reason for stress than you're feeling?
- When you're in your small group, determine the most stressful item that shows up on nearly all of your lists. Does it have financial overtones? What does that tell you about financial stresses?

PRAY

God, help me to deal with these life stresses . . .

READ Generous Gifts

2 Corinthians 8:1-4

Now, friends, I want to report on the surprising and generous
ways in which God is working in the churches in Macedonia
province. Fierce troubles came down on the people of those
churches, pushing them to the very limit. The trial exposed their
true colors: They were incredibly happy, though desperately
poor. The pressure triggered something totally unexpected: an
outpouring of pure and generous gifts. I was there and saw it for
myself. They gave offerings of whatever they could—far more
than they could afford!—pleading for the privilege of helping
out in the relief of poor Christians.

THINK

- "Incredibly happy, though desperately poor"—ever been there?
  Ever been near there? If so, what are your memories of that
  season?
- What is Paul suggesting here? That the less money you have,
  the more generous you should be? That if you give more than
  you can afford, God will take care of your needs?
- Why does the Bible on one hand minimize the importance of
  money yet on the other hand, in passages such as this one,
  seem to rate your spiritual status by your use of money?
- If you were to take the apostle's suggestions here seriously
  and act on them, what effect would it have on your family? On
  those close to you?

THINK (CONTINUED)

PRAY

Lord, give me clarity . . .

READ   The Bottom Line

From *The Shelter of Each Other*, by Mary Pipher[2]

[To those in the middle class] money is necessary for health insurance, lessons and educational opportunities. Because the community is stratified, money is necessary to keep the family in the middle class. It's necessary to buy the right clothes and bikes so that the kids won't be ostracized at school. Money is necessary to buy the violins, computers and dance lessons so that the children can have the right friends. Money is now necessary to keep families safe. And [middle-class families] are . . . worried that [their] children will be poorer than [they] are. . . .

Our current value system emphasizes profit over human well-being. Is it, as the French say, "le capitalisme sauvage," savage capitalism? Rats live by the laws of supply and demand; humans should be allowed to live by higher laws, ones that include the concepts of justice, mercy and truth. Economic laws are not the only laws of the universe. The bottom line is not the only line. Most of us are better than this belief system. We want a life organized around something besides money. Most of us do not believe that "the boy with the most toys wins in the end." Rather we hope that what will survive of us is love.

Mark 4:18-19

"The seed cast in the weeds represents the ones who hear the kingdom news but are overwhelmed with worries about all the things they have to do and all the things they want to get. The stress strangles what they heard, and nothing comes of it."

THINK

- If you consider yourself middle class, how accurately does Pipher describe how you use money to maintain your children's safety, sustain their educational opportunities, and provide for them those things you believe are necessary?
- Is Pipher being harsh on capitalism? How can one not live according to the laws of supply and demand, at least in our world today?
- Take a look at Mark's version of Jesus' words. At what point does having the things that describe the middle class become a strangling stress?
- How can you keep all you own (or the little you own) from overwhelming the kingdom news in you with worries and stress?

PRAY

Lord, keep me from being overwhelmed by . . .

READ Don't Be Obsessed

Philippians 4:11-14

Actually, I don't have a sense of needing anything personally. I've learned by now to be quite content whatever my circumstances. I'm just as happy with little as with much, with much as with little. I've found the recipe for being happy whether full or hungry, hands full or hands empty. Whatever I have, wherever I am, I can make it through anything in the One who makes me who I am. I don't mean that your help didn't mean a lot to me—it did. It was a beautiful thing that you came alongside me in my troubles.

Hebrews 13:5-6

Don't be obsessed with getting more material things. Be relaxed with what you have. Since God assured us, "I'll never let you down, never walk off and leave you," we can boldly quote,

> God is there, ready to help;
> I'm fearless no matter what.
> Who or what can get to me?

THINK

- Just because an apostle—probably unmarried, often living off the hospitality of others—claimed he didn't "have a sense of needing anything personally," does that mean you shouldn't either?
- What would have to change inside you—or in the circumstances around you—for you to be "just as happy with little as with much"?
- Paul certainly fit the model that Jesus and the Twelve lived out during their three ministry years: a spartan life when it came to possessions, but a lush life in terms of relationships. How do the spiritual leaders you know (perhaps you are one) measure up (or down) to this model?

• What biblical model is there to explain the relatively moneyed lives most American Christians live today?

PRAY

God, give me insight into . . .

READ   Empty Barns

Habakkuk 3:17-18

Though the cherry trees don't blossom
    and the strawberries don't ripen,
Though the apples are worm-eaten
    and the wheat fields stunted,
Though the sheep pens are sheepless
    and the cattle barns empty,
I'm singing joyful praise to GOD.
    I'm turning cartwheels of joy to my Savior God.

THINK

- At what point in your life should you stop trying to get more money and start "singing joyful praise to God"?
- Do you feel Habakkuk's words are divinely approved sentiments? Should we take these words as a direct command from God about how to behave in the face of financial disaster and that to behave otherwise is disobedience? Why or why not?
- What is the difference between a village idiot who when famine threatens turns cartwheels down the middle of the street and sings at the top of his voice, and a worshiper of the one true God who takes Habakkuk's words at face value?
- Is it possible that worshiping God can reduce some of the stress of a dire situation? When, if ever, have you found this to be true?

THINK (CONTINUED)

PRAY

Lord, help me to . . .

READ Seeking Contentment

From *A Minute of Margin*, by Richard A. Swenson, M.D.[3]

Our relationship to money is an area where contentment is essential. The poor envy the rich while the rich envy the richer. Money gives a thrill but no satiety. The rich soon sense this and are perhaps surprised by it but then go back to making more money anyway. Satisfaction will come later, they speculate, and if it never comes, at least there is the thrill.

Money does seem to meet our needs short term. It buys us food, shelter, vehicles, and experiences. It does not, however, meet any of our long-term needs: love, truth, relationship, redemption. This short-term deception is a tricky obstacle for us to understand and is one of the reasons God spent so much time instructing us concerning money and wealth. Money is treacherous, we are told, and riches are deceitful. It is not a sin to be wealthy, but it can be dangerous.

THINK

- Where do you fall on the "contentment" scale when it comes to your money? Do you make enough? Do you always feel like you need to make more?
- How does a lack of contentment impact your stress with finances? Where does that lack of contentment come from?
- Do you agree that "money is treacherous"? Why or why not? Why do you think God spent so much time instructing us on this topic?
- In what ways can you work toward a level of contentment that reduces your stress?

THINK (CONTINUED)

PRAY

Father, help me find contentment . . .

LIVE

What I Want to Discuss

What have you discovered this week that you definitely want to discuss with your small group? Write that here. Then begin your small-group discussion with these thoughts.

So What?

Use the following space to summarize what you've uncovered about how money worries feed your stress, along with whatever alleviating possibilities you've come across in your reading or conversation. Review your "Beginning Place" if you need to remember where you began. How does God's truth impact the "next step" in your journey?

Then What?

What is one practical thing you can do to apply what you've discovered? Describe how you would put this into practice. What steps would you take? Remember to think realistically—an admirable but unreachable goal is as good as no goal. Discuss your goal in your small group to further define it.

How?

Identify how you will be held accountable to the goal you described. Who will be on your support team? What are their responsibilities? How will you measure the success of your plan? Write the details here.

I CAN'T DO ENOUGH TO SATISFY MY WIFE

"In most ways I can think of, I'm a good and loving husband. But then why do I get this sense from her that I don't measure up—that there's always more I should be doing for her, for our marriage?"

A REMINDER:

Before you dive into this study, spend a little time reviewing what you wrote in the previous lesson's "Live" sections. How are you doing? Check with your small-group members and review your progress toward the specified goals. If necessary, adjust your goals and plans, and then recommit to them.

THE BEGINNING PLACE

Once again, I didn't sleep well. The room was too cold. My wife was too warm and the room was too cold. At forty-six, Norma is entering a phase of life that's almost as difficult for me as it is for her. She's having hot flashes, which means she insists on

A note to unmarried men: This lesson isn't just for married men. Perhaps you're dating someone—seriously or casually. Do you ever feel like you're just not doing enough in the relationship? Not being romantic enough, not living up to her expectations? Not being enough of a leader? Enough of a listener? Enough of an encourager? These are real stressors to a relationship. And they don't go away with the commitment of marriage. Join your married friends in this discussion and wrestle with what this means to you.

blasting the air conditioner all night, so every morning I wake up freezing. I wonder if I should sleep downstairs on the sofa. I wonder if I should go to a motel. But I won't leave Norma's side, even though there are icicles in my beard. I won't desert my wife, even though she's single-handedly bringing on another Ice Age in North America. There's a huge white bear pawing at our window. Because I love my wife, I will kill the bear. I will wear its fur. I will be called He Who Killed the Bear for the Love of a Perimenopausal Woman.

—FROM "SY SAFRANSKY'S NOTEBOOK," *THE SUN*, OCTOBER 2001

It's a pity that our women no longer need bears killed—or forests cleared, dwellings built, fields plowed, or furniture tooled. In those times (basically, all of human history until the last century), a man knew unambiguously how to satisfy his woman in at least the primal ways to keep his mate his, to keep his hearth warm, to give him off-spring.

Now? Women and men alike are capable of bartering personal services for dwellings, for furnishings, for food, for protection. In all the old tribal, practical ways, men and women hardly depend on each other. They don't need each other, and neither needs children. In fact, the modern American family has achieved almost a purely sentimental function. There is no longer any need for a man to take a wife (legal or common-law) or to have children. Society hardly frowns anymore on singleness, on cohabitation (straight or gay), or on childlessness (by choice or necessity).

So men don't need wives and children to keep a homestead oper-ating, yet we feel pressed by the weight of our relationships. No won-der, since we no longer spend our days working within those domestic spheres. We commute for miles and for hours to worksites, where we spend most of our waking hours—and our most alert, most productive hours, at that. It isn't surprising that we have to work so hard convinc-ing ourselves that our families, with whom we spend the least time, are the most important people to us.

Without bears to kill for our wives, what do they possibly need from us? Lifelong romancing, we're told, and understanding and leadership and partnership and security and space and . . .

You get the point. Even if your wife is not particularly demanding, expectations are so high these days, relationships so manically analyzed, that most American men can't help but feel impotent, in one way or another, when it comes to satisfying their wives.

How capable do you feel at being able to satisfy your wife? Do you think husbands have been saddled with an impossible task—to be Mr. Everything to a woman? Can any one man—any one *person*—completely satisfy another? How do your feelings of potency or impotence jibe with how you understand your faith?

Use the space below to summarize your beginning place for this lesson. Describe the realities in your quest to satisfy your wife—in particular, the realities you avoid speaking aloud with your wife. We'll start here and then go deeper.

READ The Other Woman

Genesis 16:1-6; 21:9-14

Sarai, Abram's wife, hadn't yet produced a child.

She had an Egyptian maid named Hagar. Sarai said to Abram, "GOD has not seen fit to let me have a child. Sleep with my maid. Maybe I can get a family from her." Abram agreed to do what Sarai said.

So Sarai, Abram's wife, took her Egyptian maid Hagar and gave her to her husband Abram as a wife. Abram had been living ten years in Canaan when this took place. He slept with Hagar and she got pregnant. When Hagar learned she was pregnant, she looked down on her mistress.

Sarai told Abram, "It's all your fault that I'm suffering this abuse. I put my maid in bed with you and the minute she knows she's pregnant, she treats me like I'm nothing. May GOD decide which of us is right."

"You decide," said Abram. "Your maid is your business."

Sarai was abusive to Hagar and Hagar ran away. . . .

One day Sarah saw the son that Hagar the Egyptian had borne to Abraham, poking fun at her son Isaac. She told Abraham, "Get rid of this slave woman and her son. No child of this slave is going to share inheritance with my son Isaac!"

The matter gave great pain to Abraham—after all, Ishmael was his son. But God spoke to Abraham, "Don't feel badly about the boy and your maid. Do whatever Sarah tells you. Your descendants will come through Isaac. Regarding your maid's son, be assured that I'll also develop a great nation from him—he's your son too."

Abraham got up early the next morning, got some food together and a canteen of water for Hagar, put them on her back and sent her away with the child. She wandered off into the desert of Beersheba.

THINK

- What was Abraham's dissatisfaction? What was his wife's?
- Compare this ancient way of satisfying a dissatisfied wife with modern methods. How would this narrative have played out in, say, Tulsa or Cincinnati or Hartford?
- Ever have an ex (girlfriend or wife) that kept your present marriage on edge? What price did you pay (financially, emotionally, and so on) in an attempt to satisfy them both?
- What role have children played in how well or how poorly your wife feels satisfied by you?
- If you're currently unattached, what's your take on this? Does marriage seem to intensify or alleviate a man's stress?

PRAY

Lord, show me how to . . .

READ   Unmen

From *Perhaps Women*, by Sherwood Anderson[1]

When more men worked in the fields and when most of the goods we need to cover our nakedness against the cold, the houses we live in, were made by men's hands, men were different. . . .

It is a bit absurd for me to try to make anything. I had better just sit dumbly here. The machine can make whatever I need in the common affairs of my life faster and better than I can.

My notion is that men need this direct connection with nature in work. They need to touch materials with their hands. They need to form materials, need to make things with their own hands out of wood, clay, iron, etc. They need to own tools and handle tools.

Not doing it, not being permitted to do it, does something to men. They all know it. They hate to admit it, but it is true. Not being able to do it makes them less men. They become no good for women. They spoil things for women too.

THINK

- When was the last time you created something with your hands? What are your feelings when you do?
- Where in your generational chain did your family's men stop working with their hands? Or have they?
- What might the connection be between men-making-things-with-tools and the satisfaction of their women?
- Is there evidence in Anderson's theory for blue-collar men having more success in satisfying their wives?
- Do you believe that education (not just degrees but also reading, seminars, conferences) feeds or relieves the stress men feel in trying to satisfy their wives?

THINK (CONTINUED)

PRAY

God, help me discover how to . . .

READ Faking It

Romans 12:9

Love from the center of who you are; don't fake it.

THINK

- What in your marriage are you inclined to fake? What in your marriage are you inclined to be utterly authentic about?
- What degree of self-knowledge or life experience is required before you can "love from the center of who you are"?
- Recount the last time you felt that you loved your wife "from the center of who you are."
- If you *are* faking it (whatever "it" might be) in this or that aspect of your marriage, is there any compelling reason for you to *stop*? Or do you feel that the marriage you've made or been dealt requires some faking in order to survive? Think about this.

PRAY

Father, teach me to be authentic . . .

READ Fired

From the *Business Week* article "Lost Job, Lost Spouse,"
by Margaret Popper[2]

Everyone knows that financial stress can help break up a marriage. But a new study from the National Bureau of Economic Research Inc. shows that some financial problems are more likely than others to lead to divorce.

In particular, the authors of the study, Kerwin Kofi Charles of University of Michigan and Melvin Stephens Jr. of Carnegie Mellon University, find that being fired from a job significantly raises the probability of getting divorced. Married men who are fired have an 18% higher chance of being divorced within the next three years, while women have a 13% higher chance.

But . . . a plant closing that affects a group of people doesn't raise the odds of divorce. . . . A plant closing or a sudden disability is viewed as bad luck rather than a deserved punishment for a bad personality.

THINK

- What expectations do you feel from your wife about your job?
- Have you ever been let go (fired, canned, sacked—not merely downsized)? What effect did it have on your marriage?
- Have you ever lived (or are you living now) with the threat of being fired breathing down your neck? If so, how did it affect your marriage?
- How would you feel if your wife were fired from her job? Do your wife's expectations for you regarding your job tend to be *stressful* or *encouraging?* Think about this.

THINK (CONTINUED)

PRAY

Lord, prepare me for . . .

READ Hypocrites—or Just Miserable?

From *TrueFaced*, by Bill Thrall, Bruce McNicol, and John Lynch[3]

Doug and Wanda presented a very impressive image of their relationship. They were marriage and family retreat speakers, and he taught future pastors marriage and family courses in a seminary. Yet Doug told us, "I am deeply angry with my wife. I have been for a long time. But my anger is no match for her long-standing disappointment in who I am and have become. She withdraws from me. Our physical relationship is almost nonexistent. We continually speak to scores of couples and families, but we are bluffing about our own marriage."

Question: How can a man and woman with such key responsibilities for transferring truth to others know next to nothing about applying that truth to their marriage and family? At what scale of risk does the next generation find itself when being influenced by these kinds of leaders?

THINK

- How does it strike you that a couple like this, in public ministry, is having private problems about the very thing they're supposed to be experts in? Improbable? Ironic? Hypocritical? Tragic? Perilous? Only too human?
- What do you think of the authors' implication that because Doug and Wanda don't live as they teach, they "know next to nothing about applying" their teaching to themselves?
- Do you identify to any degree with Doug's long-standing, deep anger with his wife? Or can you recall a time when you did? What were the circumstances?
- When was the last time you felt your wife's disappointment in you? What were the circumstances?

THINK (CONTINUED)

PRAY

God, help me to move . . .

READ Right There

1 Corinthians 7:17

And don't be wishing you were someplace else or with someone else. Where you are right now is God's place for you. Live and obey and love and believe right there. God, not your marital status, defines your life.

THINK

- Overheard in a pub: "The Christian neighbors and coworkers I know seem to define themselves by their marriages." What do you think the speaker means?
- To what degree do you define yourself by your marriage?
- If you are married, how might it affect your attitude or behavior if you didn't wear a wedding band?
- How would you respond to a man who says, "It's one thing for Paul to say that God, not my marital status, defines my life—but Paul wasn't married to my wife"? How do you think the apostle's statement balances with what he wrote only a few verses later, "All I am saying is that when you marry, you take on additional stress in an already stressful time, and I want to spare you if possible" (7:28)?

PRAY

God, help me to define . . .

LIVE

What I Want to Discuss

What have you discovered this week that you definitely want to discuss with your small group? Write that here. Then begin your small-group discussion with these thoughts.

So What?

Use the following space to summarize what you uncovered about feeling like you can't do enough to satisfy your wife and what you need to do to reduce the stress you feel about this. Review your "Beginning Place" if you need to remember where you began. How does God's truth impact the "next step" in your journey?

Then What?

What is one practical thing you can do to apply what you've discovered? Describe how you would put this into practice. What steps would you take? Remember to think realistically—an admirable but unreachable goal is as good as no goal. Discuss your goal in your small group to further define it.

How?

Identify how you will be held accountable to the goal you described. Who will be on your support team? What are their responsibilities? How will you measure the success of your plan? Write the details here.

MY KIDS DEMAND
TOO MUCH OF ME

"I remember when I was a child. It was nothing like
what my grandparents lived, but still—I'm doing way,
way more for my kids than was ever done for me.
I can't figure out if I'm spoiling them or
shortchanging their childhood."

A REMINDER:

*Before you dive into this study, spend a little time reviewing what you wrote in the
previous lesson's "Live" sections. How are you doing? Check with your small-group
members and review your progress toward the specified goals. If necessary, adjust
your goals and plans, and then recommit to them.*

THE BEGINNING PLACE

How many sermons, marriage-and-
family seminars, Christian books,
and "How to Parent Biblically"
talks give Christian men permission to both love their children
and feel driven up the wall by
them? Yet you know how inevita-
ble such feelings are—especially
now that most of our society is

> **A note to men without children:** Yes, this
> lesson is specifically written to men who
> have sons and daughters. But don't skip
> this lesson if you're not a father. This les-
> son is about dealing with the demands
> others place on you. Here those "others"
> are children—but many of the discover-
> able truths in this lesson can apply to
> friendships, too. Also, you may learn
> something about your own upbringing
> by going through this lesson. Look here
> for truths that can apply to your unique
> circumstances.

no longer agrarian and rural. Children are, bluntly stated, a drain on
an individual or a couple. It's a drain parents are usually happy to live
with (more during some seasons than others), yet it's still a drain—of

time, money, energy. Seldom do children contribute to the operation of the household anywhere near what their parents contribute to what we moderns call a child's "healthy development."

It is not a big jump from realizing this to feeling imposed upon, demanded of, or unappreciated—especially when your kids' friends are a click or two higher up the socioeconomic scale and you are treated to a daily inventory of what other kids have that your kids don't—their own late-model wheels, an Ivy League college education, and always more independence from parental control.

"In raising my children," one parent said, "I have lost my mind but found my soul." The first part is certainly true, you concede, but to those with young children or teenagers still in the house, the jury may still be out about the second part.

And it's often the demands those children and teenagers make on you that drive you . . . well, where? How do you cope with the demands of your children? Do they create another layer of stress for you? What's the result of this stress rippling through your marriage or primary relationships? Through your job or career? Does resenting your kids (whether a momentary pang or a lingering discomfort) make you feel like a lesser Christian?

Use the space below to summarize your beginning place for this lesson. Describe your child-induced stresses, the demands (implicit or explicit) you hear or sense from them, your reactions to them, and how they affect or are affected by your faith. We'll start here and then go deeper.

READ Stress Survey

From "The Parental Stress Scale: Initial Psychometric Evidence," by J. O. Berry and W. H. Jones[1]

Parental Stress Scale

The following statements describe feelings and perceptions about the experience of being a parent. Think of each of the items in terms of how your relationship with your child or children typically is. Please indicate the degree to which you agree or disagree with the following items by placing the appropriate number in the space provided.

1 = STRONGLY DISAGREE
2 = DISAGREE
3 = UNDECIDED
4 = AGREE
5 = STRONGLY AGREE

____ 1. I am happy in my role as a parent.

____ 2. There is little or nothing I wouldn't do for my child(ren) if it were necessary.

____ 3. Caring for my child(ren) sometimes takes more time and energy than I have to give.

____ 4. I sometimes worry whether I am doing enough for my child(ren).

____ 5. I feel close to my child(ren).

____ 6. I enjoy spending time with my child(ren).

____ 7. My child(ren) is an important source of affection for me.

____ 8. Having a child(ren) gives me a more certain and optimistic view for the future.

____ 9. The major source of stress in my life is my child(ren).

____ 10. Having a child(ren) leaves little time and flexibility in my life.

____ 11. Having a child(ren) has been a financial burden.

____ 12. It is difficult to balance different responsibilities because of my child(ren).

____ 13. The behavior of my child(ren) is often embarrassing or stressful to me.

_____ 14. If I had it to do over again, I might decide not to have a child(ren).

_____ 15. I feel overwhelmed by the responsibility of being a parent.

_____ 16. Having a child(ren) has meant having too few choices and too little control over my life.

_____ 17. I am satisfied as a parent.

_____ 18. I find my child(ren) enjoyable.

Okay, the moment of truth has arrived. To compute the parental stress score, items 1, 2, 5, 6, 7, 8, 17, and 18 should be reverse scored as follows: (1=5) (2=4) (3=3) (4=2) (5=1). Now add up your item scores. Got a total? Now identify where you land on this utterly unscientific but reasonably helpful scale:

77–90 Extreme kid-induced stress—you probably need therapy, right now (we're serious).

63–76 This level of stress will take a toll on you and your children, if it hasn't already.

47–62 Moderate stress (though this level of stress is not necessarily where most parents score).

33–46 Child-induced stress doesn't occupy much of your psyche.

18–32 You're so blissed out that we're not at all sure you're even a parent.

THINK

- Does the description next to your score feel close to the mark? What about it does? What about it doesn't?
- Did any of the eighteen items stand out as ones your child would probably have answered differently than you did? If so, which ones?
- What is your understanding of how your relationship with Christ figures into what you've learned from this exercise?

THINK (CONTINUED)

PRAY

Lord, grant me patience . . .

READ The Irresponsible Child

Luke 2:41-50

Every year Jesus' parents traveled to Jerusalem for the Feast of Passover. When he was twelve years old, they went up as they always did for the Feast. When it was over and they left for home, the child Jesus stayed behind in Jerusalem, but his parents didn't know it. Thinking he was somewhere in the company of pilgrims, they journeyed for a whole day and then began looking for him among relatives and neighbors. When they didn't find him, they went back to Jerusalem looking for him.

The next day they found him in the Temple seated among the teachers, listening to them and asking questions. The teachers were all quite taken with him, impressed with the sharpness of his answers. But his parents were not impressed; they were upset and hurt.

His mother said, "Young man, why have you done this to us? Your father and I have been half out of our minds looking for you."

He said, "Why were you looking for me? Didn't you know that I had to be here, dealing with the things of my Father?" But they had no idea what he was talking about.

THINK

- Why do you suppose there is virtually *nothing* in the New Testament about Jesus' childhood (except this one incident, of course)?
- Have you ever really pondered what it would have been like living in Jesus' family—especially as his father? If you haven't, spend some time now thinking or talking about this.
- Jesus' parents, this passage in Luke reports, "were not impressed" but were rather "upset and hurt." If you take these words at face value, how (if at all) do they revise your understanding of Jesus as a youngster?

• Do you think Jesus as a child could well have caused his parents stress? If so, how does this make you feel about the stress you may be experiencing because of your children?

PRAY

Father, lead me to . . .

READ The Damage

From the *U.S. News & World Report* article "Time Out," by John Marks[2]

Signs of stress and retreat are everywhere. Jeffrey Stiefler, the president of American Express, quit his job to "work a less intense pace and spend more time with my family." William Galston, a key adviser to President Clinton, walked away from his White House job this year after his 10-year-old son wrote him a letter: "Baseball's not fun when there's no one there to applaud you." Anna Quindlen, a high-profile columnist rumored to be the first woman in line for the top editor's job at the *New York Times*, quit her post to be home with her elementary-school-age children and write novels.

THINK

- To what degree is your child-related stress due to your job situation?
- Does your job give you the time you want with your kids? Does it prohibit you from spending the time you want with your kids? Or does it actually provide a break from the kids?
- If you earned, say, twice as much as you do now, would your parenting improve? (Be honest here, not noble.) If so, how? If not, why not?
- Have you ever suffered financially by choosing your children's welfare over your income? Explain.

PRAY

God, give me time to . . .

READ End of Your Rope

Psalm 143:1-7

> Listen to this prayer of mine, GOD;
>> pay attention to what I'm asking.
> Answer me—you're famous for your answers!
>> Do what's right for me.
> But don't, please don't, haul me into court;
>> not a person alive would be acquitted there.
>
> The enemy hunted me down;
>> he kicked me and stomped me within an inch of my life.
> He put me in a black hole,
>> buried me like a corpse in that dungeon.
> I sat there in despair, my spirit draining away,
>> my heart heavy, like lead.
> I remembered the old days,
>> went over all you've done, pondered the ways you've worked,
> Stretched out my hands to you,
>> as thirsty for you as a desert thirsty for rain.
>
> Hurry with your answer, GOD!
>> I'm nearly at the end of my rope.
> Don't turn away; don't ignore me!
>> That would be certain death.

THINK

- When was the last time your children subjected you to feelings expressed here by the psalmist? What were the circumstances?
- What phrase in particular do you most identify with when it comes to stress-inducing problems with your children?
- In the middle of parenting stresses, what proportion of the "fix" do you look to God for? What proportion do you look to yourself for? To your children?

• If you have children at home now, is your "spirit draining away"—or is your spirit in a refueling season at the moment? Talk about this. How can your relationship with God help stop the draining?

PRAY

Lord, point me toward . . .

READ Father Failures

From *Inside Out*, by Larry Crabb[3]

Perhaps the most difficult thing for many people to admit is that they feel let down by their parents. Even victims of child abuse sometimes cling to the hope that the abusing parent really loved them "but didn't know how to show it." It's hard to squarely face the fact that we have not been loved with the love we want so badly. It's been my experience in counseling that people more easily admit to their own failure to love others than to the profound disappointment a parent's love has been to them.

Many of us have wonderful parents, as I do, for whom we are deeply grateful. But all of us long for what the very best parent can never provide: perfect love that's always there with understanding, deeply and sacrificially concerned *at every moment* for our welfare, never too burdened with its own cares to be sensitive to ours, strong enough to handle a full awareness of our faults without retreating, and wise enough to direct us properly at every crossroad. No parent measures up to those standards, yet our heart will settle for nothing less. And because every child naturally turns to his primary caregiver for what he desperately wants, every child is disappointed.

From *Iron John*, by Robert Bly[4]

Some blow usually comes from the father, one way or another. . . . The wound that hurts us so much . . . we have to regard as a gift. Those with no wounds are the unluckiest of all.

THINK

- How true do you think it is that all fathers cannot help but fail their children?
- Where in you (if anywhere) lies your disappointment with a parent's love?

- When were you first aware of areas in which your parent failed or wounded you? Did recognition come out of the blue in an ordinary day, or did it take a crisis to open you up to this epiphany?
- Do these quotes add more stress to your fathering duties, or do they actually relieve some of the stress? What have you heard taught from the Bible along these lines? Do you feel it generally agrees or disagrees with this pair of quotes?

PRAY

God, show me . . .

READ   Take It in Stride

1 Peter 4:12-13,19

Friends, when life gets really difficult, don't jump to the conclusion that God isn't on the job. Instead, be glad that you are in the very thick of what Christ experienced. This is a spiritual refining process, with glory just around the corner. . . .

So if you find life difficult because you're doing what God said, take it in stride. Trust him. He knows what he's doing, and he'll keep on doing it.

THINK

- What conclusions do you jump to when feeling stressed by your children?
- What kind of glory is lurking just around the corner related to your parenting? And what is that corner?
- How do you feel when someone tells you that the misery you're experiencing is actually a "spiritual refining process"?
- Are *all* your parenting difficulties from the hand of God, who "knows what he's doing"? If not all, how can you know which difficulties are from God and which ones aren't? Does it even matter?

PRAY

God, redirect me where necessary . . .

LIVE

What I Want to Discuss

What have you discovered this week that you definitely want to discuss with your small group? Write that here. Then begin your small-group discussion with these thoughts.

So What?

Use the following space to summarize what you uncovered about the stress you feel from your kids' demands and what you need to do so you neither resent your children nor abdicate your role as father. Review your "Beginning Place" if you need to remember where you began. How does God's truth impact the "next step" in your journey?

Then What?

What is one practical thing you can do to apply what you've discovered? Describe how you would put this into practice. What steps would you take? Remember to think realistically—an admirable but unreachable goal is as good as no goal. Discuss your goal in your small group to further define it.

How?

Identify how you will be held accountable to the goal you described. Who will be on your support team? What are their responsibilities? How will you measure the success of your plan? Write the details here.

WHO'S LOOKING OUT FOR ME?

"With all the people I seem to be taking care of,
it'd be nice once in a while to feel that
someone was watching out for me."

A REMINDER:

Before you dive into this study, spend a little time reviewing what you wrote in the previous lesson's "Live" sections. How are you doing? Check with your small-group members and review your progress toward the specified goals. If necessary, adjust your goals and plans, and then recommit to them.

THE BEGINNING PLACE

"I'm watching your six." "I'll run interference." "Who's the point man?" "I'd take a bullet for you."

The metaphors men use to describe their relational support systems come largely from sports and combat. The only trouble is, too often it's *only* in sports and combat that a man knows true protection, feels covered, trusts that a buddy would put it all on the line for him.

Meanwhile, in the civilian world, we tend to fall back on "God Is My Copilot" reasoning: after all, what good is a frail human to depend on? Jesus is the only reliable partner, friend, comrade.

Or is he? The prime, the most reliable, the eternal—of course. But the *only* reliable? Christian teaching is long on intimacy with Jesus but short on how to nurture the kind of intimacy with another human that covers you, that prompts a friend to call you and ask how *you're* doing. Some think it's just another facet of that deep-seated American male fear of "meddling" in another man's private business or personal affairs. The best we usually can do is hint vaguely at our dark sides without actually naming anything or anyone. Consequently, more often than not we are not known, and we do not know ourselves or other men.

Small wonder we feel isolated in crowded workplaces, and despite the advice of the Dr. Phils and James Dobsons—of self-help gurus on TV and on the shelves of Barnes & Noble—we are too often stressed by the loneliness of it all. Especially if your job is a ministry job, which typically demands that you look out for everyone else, bodies as well as souls.

What about you? Do you feel isolated about issues that really matter to you? Have you hung up the phone after talking someone through a horrific stretch and asked yourself, *Who could I call in a moment of crisis?* What effect does your relationship with Christ have on this kind of stress?

Use the space below to summarize your beginning place for this lesson. Describe what isolation (social, emotional, spiritual, physical) you may be feeling or that you feel on occasion, what kind of stress this kind of isolation produces in you, and what you understand the Bible has to say about it, if anything. We'll start here and then go deeper.

READ Loneliness

From CyberParent.com

Certainly marriage is no cure for loneliness. . . . Married men with successful, vibrant careers—"real men" by anyone's standards—often feel isolated and apart, even in marriage and family life. This is what a few had to say:

"My kids don't talk to me the way they do to my wife. I feel excluded."

"I always have to be the strong father-image and keep order in the troops. Even when I am with my wife and kids, I often feel apart from them."

"My wife and I have lots of friends. But they are really her friends and her friends' husbands. Sometimes I feel apart from the whole group."

"Ever since I was a child I have had this feeling of apartness. I had good parents and I have a wonderful wife. I just feel apart from other people. Why, I don't know."

THINK

- Have you ever felt, if not voiced, this wistful puzzlement about yourself: a good upbringing, wonderful wife—yet a feeling of apartness, of loneliness?
- Does your job tend to feed or cure a sense of isolation? Explain.
- How easily do you make good friends? Are they the sort you primarily play with, work with, or simply hang with?
- Do you have at least one friend with whom you can express your deepest thoughts? If so, how did you grow this kind of friendship? If not, how can you develop one? What is the greatest value of having a friend like this?

THINK (CONTINUED)

PRAY

God, lead me to find . . .

READ   We Haven't Broken

2 Corinthians 4:8-9,16-18

You know for yourselves that we're not much to look at. We've been surrounded and battered by troubles, but we're not demoralized; we're not sure what to do, but we know that God knows what to do; we've been spiritually terrorized, but God hasn't left our side; we've been thrown down, but we haven't broken. . . .

So we're not giving up. How could we! Even though on the outside it often looks like things are falling apart on us, on the inside, where God is making new life, not a day goes by without his unfolding grace. These hard times are small potatoes compared to the coming good times, the lavish celebration prepared for us. There's far more here than meets the eye. The things we see now are here today, gone tomorrow. But the things we can't see now will last forever.

THINK

- When, if ever, have you noticed, studied, or lingered on these verses?
- What aspects or phrases in this excerpt of Paul's letter resonate most deeply with you or connect most immediately with you?
- What aspects or phrases puzzle you most?
- Where in these words (if anywhere) is there hope for men worn down by looking out for everyone else?
- "There's far more here than meets the eye." What do these words of the apostle say to you?

THINK (CONTINUED)

PRAY

God, bring me to a place . . .

READ Following a Cloud

Numbers 9:15-23

The day The Dwelling was set up, the Cloud covered The Dwelling of the Tent of Testimony. From sunset until daybreak it was over The Dwelling. It looked like fire. It was like that all the time, the Cloud over The Dwelling and at night looking like fire.

When the Cloud lifted above the Tent, the People of Israel marched out; and when the Cloud descended the people camped. The People of Israel marched at GOD's command and they camped at his command. As long as the Cloud was over The Dwelling, they camped. Even when the Cloud hovered over The Dwelling for many days, they honored GOD's command and wouldn't march. They stayed in camp, obedient to GOD's command, as long as the Cloud was over The Dwelling, but the moment GOD issued orders they marched. If the Cloud stayed only from sunset to daybreak and then lifted at daybreak, they marched. Night or day, it made no difference—when the Cloud lifted, they marched. It made no difference whether the Cloud hovered over The Dwelling for two days or a month or a year, as long as the Cloud was there, they were there. And when the Cloud went up, they got up and marched. They camped at GOD's command and they marched at GOD's command. They lived obediently by GOD's orders as delivered by Moses.

From *Inside Out*, by Larry Crabb[1]

Think about what actually must have happened: thousands of Israelites trudging through a tedious desert, some probably ill, others feeling energetic, still others bothered by leg cramps. I can picture one out-of-shape, middle-aged father of four puffing along, yelling at his kids to stop bickering, worried about the chest pains that get worse the more he walks. He glances up regularly to see if the cloud is showing any sign of slowing down and feels annoyed as he watches it floating on ahead.

"Whoever is blowing that cloud along," he grumbles under his breath, "sure doesn't know what I'm going through—or else He doesn't care. My wife can't handle the kids, my angina is kicking up—we need a break. I have to stop or I'm going to collapse. Please, Lord, stop the cloud." But it keeps on moving.

An hour or two passes by and, strangely, his chest pains stop. He feels a burst of energy, sort of a "runner's high." His older boy is carrying the tired toddler. He looks over at his wife and she's grinning. "Maybe God knew continued walking was the best thing for all of us." He feels a new bounce in his steps—and just then the cloud stops.

The man looks up in puzzled disgust, unable to understand what's happening. "When I'm too tired to continue, God makes me press on. When I feel like covering ground, I'm told to take a break."

With the rest of the crowd, he obediently stops, unloads the animals, and sets up camp. When he stretches out on a blanket, he begins to realize how badly he needed the rest. Fatigue sweeps through his body, and he gratefully yawns and closes his eyes.

Just as he dozes peacefully into the first stages of a deep sleep, his wife shakes him awake: "The cloud started moving. We've got to get going again."

Perhaps my story is a bit fanciful (certainly the biblical text includes no such record), but with the number of people whose pace was directed by that cloud, there must have been at least a few, perhaps many, who felt insensitively treated.

The way God arranges things sometimes seems uniquely designed to frustrate us: a tire goes flat on the way to the hospital; the sink backs up an hour before overnight company arrives; a friend lets you down during a time when you most need support; you suddenly develop laryngitis the day of your presentation to important buyers. In times of frustration, our High Priest sometimes seems more callous to our needs than sympathetic.

We pray, asking God to hear our cry, pleading with Him

to let nothing else go wrong. I wonder if sometimes the passion in our prayers reflects more of a *demand* than a *petition*. Frustration is excellent soil for growing a demanding spirit. It is therefore important that we handle difficulties well, allowing them to mature us rather than to push us toward demandingness.

THINK

- Does it irritate you or encourage you to hear (as you do from Crabb in his retelling) that your severe and recurring frustration can be part of God's plans for you?
- When does God expect you to "handle difficulties well" and let them mature you, and when does he expect you to pray with the faith of a mustard seed that your mountainous problems can be removed outright?
- Do you have anyone (besides God) whose care and concern for you can be irritating or frustrating? Do you more often appreciate or resent such care?
- How does God look out for his people these days? How do you wish he would demonstrate his care for you in the everyday?

PRAY

Lord, show me that you care by . . .

READ Don't Get Worked Up

Matthew 6:31-34

"What I'm trying to do here is to get you to relax, to not be so preoccupied with *getting*, so you can respond to God's *giving*. People who don't know God and the way he works fuss over these things, but you know both God and how he works. Steep your life in God-reality, God-initiative, God-provisions. Don't worry about missing out. You'll find all your everyday human concerns will be met.

"Give your entire attention to what God is doing right now, and don't get worked up about what may or may not happen tomorrow. God will help you deal with whatever hard things come up when the time comes."

THINK

- If you believed that part of what Jesus was trying to do with you is get you to relax, how would it change your day? Your thoughts? Your heart?

- Has it ever appeared to you that "all your everyday human concerns" were *not* met? How do you explain this?

- In what ways does Jesus' emphasis on the present seem at odds with popular teaching and preaching about planning for your future?

- How would your daily routine change if you steeped "your life in God-reality, God-initiative, God-provisions"? Do these words have their intended effect on you? Do they get you to relax? If not, why not?

THINK (CONTINUED)

PRAY

God, teach me how to relax . . .

READ Isolation = Higher Risk of Heart Attack?

From the American Heart Association release "Men's Social Isolation Linked to Higher Heart Disease Risk" as reported in Cardiology Online's website

Older men who have few personal relationships may have increased risk of heart disease, according to a report presented at the American Heart Association's Scientific Sessions 2003.

In a study examining factors that influence successful aging, researchers found that among a group of men in their 70s, social isolation was linked to increased levels of C-reactive protein (CRP), interleukin-6 (IL-6) and fibrinogen in the blood.

People with elevated CRP and fibrinogen have higher risks for heart disease and stroke.

"Social isolation may influence these different inflammatory markers and may be one way social relationships influence our health," said lead author Eric B. Loucks, Ph.D., research fellow at Harvard School of Public Health in Boston.

Social relationships have been linked to better health and protection against heart disease in many studies. However, the unanswered question is how social relationships translate into biological processes that affect a person's health.

Loucks and his colleagues . . . investigated CRP, IL-6 and fibrinogen as potential biological links between friends, family and health. [Questionnaire] questions included marital status, the number of close friends and family members, and the extent of religious and social club participation.

Researchers failed to find any correlation between the degree of social isolation in women and their levels of the inflammatory biomarkers.

"Men may respond differently than women to social relationships," Loucks said.

THINK

- Does the conclusion of this study seem surprising, or is it predictable? Why?
- The subjects of this experiment were men in their seventies. Do you think a study of men in their thirties and forties would render similar results? Why or why not?
- Why do you think the health of women isn't as affected by their social connectedness?
- How might stress be the connector between a man's friendlessness (we mean a lack of real, transparent, honest-to-goodness friends—not mere acquaintances) and heart disease?
- Does this study compel you toward a change in your relationships? Explain.

PRAY

God, connect me . . .

READ Take the Mercy

John 14:27

"I'm leaving you well and whole. That's my parting gift to you. Peace. I don't leave you the way you're used to being left—feeling abandoned, bereft. So don't be upset. Don't be distraught."

Hebrews 4:15-16

We don't have a priest who is out of touch with our reality. He's been through weakness and testing, experienced it all—all but the sin. So let's walk right up to him and get what he is so ready to give. Take the mercy, accept the help.

THINK

- Was there ever a time when you walked right up to Jesus and got "what he is so ready to give"? Explain that time and what you got.
- When you are feeling abandoned, how do you feel about these words from Jesus: "Don't be upset. Don't be distraught"?
- What does it mean to you that Jesus has "been through weakness and testing," has "experienced it all"?
- When you're stressed by having no one looking out for you, is "peace" answer enough for you? Why or why not? In a practical way this week, how can you "take the mercy, accept the help"?

PRAY

Father, give me mercy . . .

LIVE

What I Want to Discuss

What have you discovered this week that you definitely want to discuss with your small group? Write that here. Then begin your small-group discussion with these thoughts.

So What?

Use the following space to summarize what you've discovered about your need to be looked out for as you look out for others and what you can do to reduce your sense of isolation. Review your "Beginning Place" if you need to remember where you began. How does God's truth impact the "next step" in your journey?

Then What?

What is one practical thing you can do to apply what you've discovered? Describe how you would put this into practice. What steps would you take? Remember to think realistically—an admirable but unreachable goal is as good as no goal. Discuss your goal in your small group to further define it.

How?

Identify how you will be held accountable to the goal you described. Who will be on your support team? What are their responsibilities? How will you measure the success of your plan? Write the details here.

I'M NOT HOLDING UP MY END OF A FRIENDSHIP

"If he's as good a friend as I say he is, why is it that he always calls me and I never call him? I hate that, but I always feel too busy to call."

A REMINDER:

Before you dive into this study, spend a little time reviewing what you wrote in the previous lesson's "Live" sections. How are you doing? Check with your small-group members and review your progress toward the specified goals. If necessary, adjust your goals and plans, and then recommit to them.

THE BEGINNING PLACE

You know the type: She has a Christmas card list longer than your grandmother's; she flies to visit college and even high school friends who live on the opposite coast; it's been two decades since she's been in school, but she still nurtures those friendships as deliberately as she loves the friends.

She may be your sister, your wife, your cousin, a colleague. Whoever it is, you can't figure out where she finds the time to keep up with friends from so long ago. Meanwhile, you stumble over the names of men in your support group after missing a single week. Your mind is so used to focusing on only what's in front of you that when papers or problems or people are removed from your vision for awhile, they fade from your mind, too.

Does this seem familiar? Derek used to live near this friend of his, even worked with him—so he saw his friend a lot, accumulating a history of shared pain and joy along the way. Then Derek's friend moved away. They kept up with each other's lives for a while, but then enough time had elapsed between calls or e-mails that he realized it would take a long communiqué to bring his friend up to speed. So he kept putting it off, thinking that such a close friend deserved more than a quick note. However, what with his work pressures and church activities and youth soccer, he kept putting it off until it became clear it would take a *War and Peace*–sized tome to bring the friend up to speed. (Derek had moved twice and added a new child to the family, among other milestones.) The guilt fed his stress, which only made it less likely that he would ever contact his friend.

In such a manner, a man inadvertently puts a friendship on ice. And you are only too aware that such well-meaning estrangement doesn't require distance.

What makes it difficult for you to stay in touch with close friends? What do you need, or what do you need to do, to hold up your end of a valuable friendship? Use the space below to summarize your beginning place for this lesson. Describe the friendships you've left hanging, the stress that might have caused that situation, and the stress that piles up the longer you put off connecting with those friends. We'll start here and then go deeper.

READ Jump into the Water

From *Abba's Child*, by Brennan Manning[1]

Suppose for a moment that in a flash of insight you discovered that all your motives for ministry were essentially egocentric, or suppose that last night you got drunk and committed adultery, or suppose that you failed to respond to a cry for help and the person committed suicide. What would you do?

Would guilt, self-condemnation, and self-hatred consume you, or would you jump into the water and swim a hundred yards at breakneck speed toward Jesus? Haunted by feelings of unworthiness, would you allow the darkness to overcome you or would you let Jesus be who He is—a Savior of boundless compassion and infinite patience, a Lover who keeps no score of our wrongs?

THINK

- Describe an incident or a season where you and a close friend were bound together on one side or another of what Manning describes in the first paragraph.
- What's stopping you right now—or tomorrow, at the latest—from picking up the friendship where you left it instead of waiting until you're blindsided by the announcement of a crisis in your friend's life?
- To what degree is pride keeping you from holding up your end of a friendship?

PRAY

Lord, help me to reach out . . .

READ A Friend Like a Brother?

Genesis 27:41-45; 32:3-9,11,20-21; 33:1,3-9

Esau seethed in anger against Jacob because of the blessing his father had given [Jacob]; he brooded, "The time for mourning my father's death is close. And then I'll kill my brother Jacob."

When these words of her older son Esau were reported to Rebekah, she called her younger son Jacob and said, "Your brother Esau is plotting vengeance against you. He's going to kill you. Son, listen to me. Get out of here. Run for your life to Haran, to my brother Laban. Live with him for a while until your brother cools down, until his anger subsides and he forgets what you did to him. I'll then send for you and bring you back. Why should I lose both of you the same day?" . . .

[Twenty years and a big family later]

Then Jacob sent messengers on ahead to his brother Esau in the land of Seir in Edom. He instructed them: "Tell my master Esau this, 'A message from your servant Jacob: I've been staying with Laban and couldn't get away until now. I've acquired cattle and donkeys and sheep; also men and women servants. I'm telling you all this, my master, hoping for your approval.'"

The messengers came back to Jacob and said, "We talked to your brother Esau and he's on his way to meet you. But he has four hundred men with him."

Jacob was scared. Very scared. Panicked, he divided his people, sheep, cattle, and camels into two camps. He thought, "If Esau comes on the first camp and attacks it, the other camp has a chance to get away."

And then Jacob prayed, "God of my father Abraham, God of my father Isaac, GOD who told me, 'Go back to your parents' homeland and I'll treat you well.' . . . Save me, please, from the violence of my brother, my angry brother! I'm afraid he'll come and attack us all, me, the mothers and the children." . . .

He thought, "I will soften him up with the succession of gifts. Then when he sees me face-to-face, maybe he'll be glad to welcome me."

So his gifts went before him while he settled down for the night in the camp. . . .

Jacob looked up and saw Esau coming with his four hundred men. . . . He led the way and, as he approached his brother, bowed seven times, honoring his brother. But Esau ran up and embraced him, held him tight and kissed him. And they both wept.

Then Esau looked around and saw the women and children: "And who are these with you?"

Jacob said, "The children that God saw fit to bless me with."

Then the maidservants came up with their children and bowed; then Leah and her children, also bowing; and finally, Joseph and Rachel came up and bowed to Esau.

Esau then asked, "And what was the meaning of all those herds that I met?"

"I was hoping that they would pave the way for my master to welcome me."

Esau said, "Oh, brother. I have plenty of everything—keep what is yours for yourself."

THINK

- What indications of friendship did you detect in Jacob and Esau's otherwise fraternal relationship? How is their relationship like or unlike your friendships?
- When was the last time you asked God—maybe with some desperation—for help with a strained friendship?
- It was twenty years before these brothers saw each other again, by which time their hard feelings had thawed. But if they had had the opportunity—like living closer to each other—do you think they would have reconciled earlier? Why or why not? What does your answer say about the way you relate to friends?

THINK (CONTINUED)

PRAY

God, give me wisdom in relationships . . .

READ The Value of Friendship

From "The Dangers of Loneliness," by Hara Estroff Marano[2]

Friendship is a lot like food. We need it to survive. What is more, we seem to have a basic drive for it. Psychologists find that human beings have fundamental need for inclusion in group life and for close relationships. We are truly social animals.

The upshot is, we function best when this social need is met. It is easier to stay motivated, to meet the varied challenges of life.

In fact, evidence has been growing that when our need for social relationships is not met, we fall apart mentally and even physically. There are effects on the brain and on the body. Some effects work subtly, through the exposure of multiple body systems to excess amounts of the hormones of stress. Yet the effects are distinct enough to be measured over time, so that unmet social needs take a serious toll on health, eroding our arteries, creating high blood pressure, and even undermining learning and memory.

THINK

- How can the motivation offered by friends actually help to reduce your stress? How can your friends' involvement in your life increase your stress?
- In what ways do unmet social needs contribute to your stress?
- Which seems like a greater pressure to you: the pressure caused by having lots of friends (or demanding friends), or the pressure caused by not having many friends?
- If it is true we need friendship to survive, does that presume we have to take the stresses of friendship along with the sustenance? If so, how do you do that?

THINK (CONTINUED)

PRAY

Lord, help me to appreciate . . .

READ A Little Friendly Advice

Psalm 36:10

> Keep on loving your friends;
>> do your work in welcoming hearts.

Proverbs 14:10

> The person who shuns the bitter moments of friends
>> will be an outsider at their celebrations.

Proverbs 25:25

> Like a cool drink of water when you're worn out and weary
>> is a letter from a long-lost friend.

Ecclesiastes 4:9-12

> It's better to have a partner than go it alone.
> Share the work, share the wealth.
> And if one falls down, the other helps,
> But if there's no one to help, tough!
>
> Two in a bed warm each other.
> Alone, you shiver all night.
>
> By yourself you're unprotected.
> With a friend you can face the worst.
> Can you round up a third?
> A three-stranded rope isn't easily snapped.

THINK

- Respond to this remark: "Not keeping up your end of a friend-ship may be subtly selfish. How do you know there isn't work in someone's heart that only you can tool?"

- Not that you'd be one who knowingly "shuns the bitter moments of friends," but could falling out of regular communication with them cause you to at least *miss* the bitter moments?
- Describe your feelings when you once heard from a long-lost friend.
- What "worst" did you once face without a friend? *With* a friend? What "worst" in a friend's life did you show up for? What kind of literal or figurative protection did you give him?

PRAY

God, help me to live wisely . . .

READ Deep Friends

Romans 12:10-11,15

> Be good friends who love deeply; practice playing second fiddle.
>   Don't burn out; keep yourselves fueled and aflame. . . .
>   Laugh with your happy friends when they're happy; share
> tears when they're down.

Philippians 2:1-3

> If you've gotten anything at all out of following Christ, if his love
> has made any difference in your life, if being in a community
> of the Spirit means anything to you, if you have a heart, if you
> *care*—then do me a favor: Agree with each other, love each other,
> be deep-spirited friends. Don't push your way to the front; don't
> sweet-talk your way to the top. Put yourself aside, and help oth-
> ers get ahead.

THINK

- Is it more deliberate or coincidental that Paul's mandate to "be good friends" is followed as it is? What are the connections between having a good friend, burning out, and keeping one-self "fueled and aflame"?
- "You'll never be a good friend until you're good at playing sec-ond fiddle." Agree or disagree? Explain.
- What happens when you laugh with friends but don't cry with them? When you cry with other friends, but don't laugh with them?
- What apparently was the apostle's idea behind being "deep-spirited friends"? What does being "deep-spirited friends" imply to you?

THINK (CONTINUED)

PRAY

Father, help me to be a deep-spirited friend . . .

READ The New Friend

From *Outwitting Stress*, by Nancy Rosenberg[3]

Love your old friends—cherish them and call them and write them notes and send them flowers when they are sick. But never shut the door on making new friends.

It's easy to settle in with the bunch of friends you have, where you know each other well and the stories never change. You have your routines, your habits, your set patterns of relating. The relationships are well-worn and comfortable, like an old pair of shoes.

Let's stick with this metaphor for a while. You've got a closetful of comfortable old shoes, but you'd really like a new pair. A new pair of shoes can add color and sparkle to your wardrobe. A new friend can add color and sparkle to your life. There's an amazing quote that I have taped above my desk:

> *Each friend represents a world in us, a world not born until they arrive.*
>
> —Anaïs Nin

A new friend tells you stories you've never heard, listens to your stories with a fresh ear, and has ideas and perspectives that you may not have considered. Once you get beyond the first stages of developing a new friendship, when you get to the point where you can discuss things that really matter, the issues and concerns in your life—the things that cause you stress—a new friend will bring to the table an entirely new set of problem-solving skills. New friends can help you solve your problems, and you can help them solve theirs.

THINK

- What was a profound but hidden world in you that took a friend to reveal?
- Describe a relatively recent friendship you created from scratch and the likelihood of it becoming a close friendship.
- Picture some of your friends. Do you ever wonder how deep these friendships *really* are? What makes you wonder that?
- What practical value would there be in making a new friend? How would you go about it?

PRAY

God, lead me to new friendships . . .

LIVE

What I Want to Discuss

What have you discovered this week that you definitely want to discuss with your small group? Write that here. Then begin your small-group discussion with these thoughts.

So What?

Use the following space to summarize what you've uncovered about the stress caused by keeping a friend on the back burner. Review your "Beginning Place" if you need to remember where you began. How does God's truth impact the "next step" in your journey?

Then What?

What is one practical thing you can do to apply what you've discovered? Describe how you would put this into practice. What steps would you take? Remember to think realistically—an admirable but unreachable goal is as good as no goal. Discuss your goal in your small group to further define it.

How?

Identify how you will be held accountable to the goal you described. Who will be on your support team? What are their responsibilities? How will you measure the success of your plan? Write the details here.

MY LEASH
IS TOO SHORT

"I'll be shaving and catch my own eye and think, I'm tied back somehow. I need to stretch, but how? And stretch into what? The older I get, the more I feel this."

A REMINDER:

Before you dive into this study, spend a little time reviewing what you wrote in the previous lesson's "Live" sections. How are you doing? Check with your small-group members and review your progress toward the specified goals. If necessary, adjust your goals and plans, and then recommit to them.

THE BEGINNING PLACE

Let us first recognize the obvious and then get beyond it. A leash can protect, restrain in the presence of peril, and be a training tool. A leash is valuable, even necessary—but let us accept different lengths of leash for different people at different places in life.

All this to say, it may not be persnickety rebellion that makes you strain against some of your leashes, especially if those leashes are constraining instead of protective. Workplace leashes take the form of a micromanaging manager, a parental supervisor, or just a garden-variety control freak. Or the tightness you feel may be interior—you know you can do more, perform better, soar higher, but your own insecurities or fears rein you in.

And what about faith? Have you lately—or for a decade or more—been feeling the tug of a religious, ecclesiastical, or spiritual leash? Not a tug toward something but a tug away from something—a something you yearn for, a reality or possibility you might not be able to name but nevertheless can't forget or shrug off. All you know is that your good old religious coat is beginning to feel tight and ill fitting. You feel as though you've been marching for years and wonder if it's time to start dancing instead. You've been toying with the idea of taking all your beliefs off the shelf and giving them a good cleaning before restoring them to the shelf—but maybe not all of them, and certainly in a different arrangement.

Tight leashes, weights on your feet—these can't help but create stress in you. What are your leashes and weights and reins? Who controls them? What desires are tantalizingly just out of reach? What would you do if your leash was cut or even just lengthened some?

Use the space below to summarize your beginning place for this lesson. Describe as well as you can what leashes are holding you back and from what. We'll start here and then go deeper.

READ Shifting Your Self-Definition

From *Stress Passages*, by L. John Mason[1]

Most working people, especially men, are at their peak earning years during midlife, but often they find that making lots of money does not bring the happiness of satisfaction it did when they were younger. Midlife men often shift their self-definition away from simple job identification and want to expand their personalities. They may become more sensitive, nurturing, and dependent on social contacts. Some men take on leadership roles and find younger protégés with whom to share their business insights and experiences.

THINK

- Where would you say you are in your income-earning curve?
- To what degree do your self-definition and job identification overlap? How do you feel about that?
- If you do see some of yourself in this excerpt's description, how could others benefit from your personal evolution?
- How is a decision to shift your self-definition away from "simple job identification" a way of letting out the slack in your work life? How can you do this?

PRAY

Father, help me at work by . . .

READ   A Recovered Life

Matthew 11:28-30

"Are you tired? Worn out? Burned out on religion? Come to me. Get away with me and you'll recover your life. I'll show you how to take a real rest. Walk with me and work with me—watch how I do it. Learn the unforced rhythms of grace. I won't lay anything heavy or ill-fitting on you. Keep company with me and you'll learn to live freely and lightly."

THINK

- What in these words of Jesus resonates most deeply in you?
- What here puzzles you, seems out of place?
- How do you balance Christian teaching about the labor of spiritual growth—the deliberate and often difficult discipline of obeying God—and this message encouraging us to learn the "unforced rhythms of grace"?
- What would it look like if you actually walked and worked with Jesus?

PRAY

Lord, show me the unforced rhythms of grace . . .

READ Under Pressure

From *Stress Passages*, by Brian Chichester, et al.[2]

"If you have a jerk for a boss, there's little that you can do to keep your adrenal gland from going off regularly, but the real issue is how to cope," says Jim Laird, Ph.D., professor of psychology at Clark University in Worcester, Massachusetts, who studies emotions and stress.

"If you're constantly exposed to this type of stress, you might think that there's nothing you can do," Dr. Laird says. "But there's always a choice. Ultimately, you can leave your job. Or you can do a rational assessment of your life and maybe realize that your boss is worth putting up with for the money." . . .

Changing careers is scary. But "the vast majority of people who leave something that's depressing them wind up happier and most often financially better-off in the end," says international creativity consultant Dr. McGee-Cooper. "Don't be fooled by what seems like a difficult job market. There will always be a market for talented people with imagination and a sense of purpose."

THINK

- Does the thought of changing your job or career energize or terrify you?
- Have you or someone you know well evaluated a short-leash job, and—all things considered—decided to stay and endure the short leash? How did things turn out?
- Could it be the will of God for a Christian to *stay* in a job whose supervisor reins him in tight, micromanages him, or doesn't recognize his talent? Explain.
- Have you or someone you know well ever fled such a job? What were the immediate results? Longer-term results?

THINK (CONTINUED)

PRAY

God, release the pressure . . .

READ   Shadows

Colossians 2:16-17

So don't put up with anyone pressuring you in details of diet,
worship services, or holy days. All those things are mere shad-
ows cast before what was to come; the substance is Christ.

THINK

- What details of diet, worship services, and holy days do you
  suppose Paul was referring to?
- How do your spiritual influences (church, Bible study group,
  Christian friends) impact the way you view diet, worship, or
  holy days?
- How are restrictions, qualifiers, and rules (tacit as well as spo-
  ken) about diet and worship like a leash on your spirituality?
  What might such a leash keep you back from?
- Recall and describe the least-leashed, most free worshiping
  group or experience you've had.

PRAY

Lord, give me direction so I can . . .

READ Joy in the Present

Ecclesiastes 4:7-8; 5:15-20

I turned my head and saw yet another wisp of smoke on its way to nothingness: a solitary person, completely alone—no children, no family, no friends—yet working obsessively late into the night, compulsively greedy for more and more, never bothering to ask, "Why am I working like a dog, never having any fun? And who cares?" More smoke. A bad business. . . .

> He arrived naked from the womb of his mother;
> He'll leave in the same condition—with nothing.
> This is bad luck, for sure—naked he came, naked he went.
> So what was the point of working for a salary of smoke?
> All for a miserable life spent in the dark?

After looking at the way things are on this earth, here's what I've decided is the best way to live: Take care of your-self, have a good time, and make the most of whatever job you have for as long as God gives you life. And that's about it. That's the human lot. Yes, we should make the most of what God gives, both the bounty and the capacity to enjoy it, accept-ing what's given and delighting in the work. It's God's gift! God deals out joy in the present, the *now*. It's useless to brood over how long we might live.

THINK

- In what ways do you relate to the person who awoke "naked from the womb"?
- Who do you tend to blame more for an excessive work-load—your boss or yourself? Why?
- How, if at all, can you make the most of your present job? Your marriage? Your parenting? Your other relationships?

- How does making the most of your life tighten the leash? How does it release the leash?
- Respond to this quote: "God deals out joy in the present, the now."

PRAY

Father, grant me joy today . . .

READ One Game, at Least

From *Abba's Child*, by Brennan Manning[3]

[The child Mordecai, born to pious Jewish parents, was too rambunctious to settle down to his studies of the Scriptures. When he should have been in synagogue, he instead escaped to walk in the woods, swim in the lake, and climb trees. When the attempts of psychoanalysts and behavior modificationists to straighten out Mordecai failed,] his parents grieved for their beloved son. There seemed to be no hope.

At this same time the Great Rabbi visited the village. And the parents said, "Ah! Perhaps the Rabbi." So they took Mordecai to the Rabbi and told him their tale of woe. The Rabbi bellowed, "Leave the boy with me, and I will have a talking with him."

It was bad enough that Mordecai would not go to the synagogue. But to leave their beloved son alone with this lion of a man was terrifying. However, they had come this far, and so they left him.

Now Mordecai stood in the hallway, and the Great Rabbi stood in his parlor. He beckoned, "Boy, come here." Trembling, Mordecai came forward.

And then the Great Rabbi picked him up and held him silently against his heart.

His parents came to get Mordecai, and they took him home. The next day he went to the synagogue to learn the Word of God. And when he was done, he went to the woods. And the Word of God became one with the words of the woods, which became one with the words of Mordecai. And he swam in the lake. And the Word of God became one with the words of the lake, which became one with the words of Mordecai. And he climbed the trees. And the Word of God became one with the words of the trees, which became one with the words of Mordecai.

And Mordecai himself grew up to become a great man. People who were seized with panic came to him and found peace. People who were without anybody came to him and found communion. People with no exits came to him and found a way out. And when they came to him he said, "I first learned the Word of God when the Great Rabbi held me silently against his heart."

THINK

- What "leash" was restraining the child Mordecai?
- When, if ever, have you felt the restraint of such a leash?
- Did you first learn the heart of God or the Word of God? Recount the experience.
- Do you feel you were once held by a "Great Rabbi"? Describe this time.
- How can God's Word help you feel less held back by a leash?

PRAY

God, remove my leash . . .

LIVE

What I Want to Discuss

What have you discovered this week that you definitely want to discuss with your small group? Write that here. Then begin your small-group discussion with these thoughts.

So What?

Use the following space to summarize what you've uncovered about being reined in on a leash and the stress it causes you. Review your "Beginning Place" if you need to remember where you began. How does God's truth impact the "next step" in your journey?

Then What?

What is one practical thing you can do to apply what you've discovered? Describe how you would put this into practice. What steps would you take? Remember to think realistically—an admirable but unreachable goal is as good as no goal. Discuss your goal in your small group to further define it.

How?

Identify how you will be held accountable to the goal you described. Who will be on your support team? What are their responsibilities? How will you measure the success of your plan? Write the details here.

HOPE

"Juggling still, but on flat ground—and without chainsaws."

A TIME TO REVIEW

We come to the final lesson in our *Juggling Chainsaws on a Tightrope* discussion guide, but this is not an ending place. Hopefully, you've been discovering some truths about your life and seen opportunity for change—positive change. But no matter what has brought you to lesson 8, you know that it's only a pause in your journey.

You may have uncovered behaviors or thoughts that demanded change. Perhaps you've already changed them. Will the changes stick? How will you continue to take the momentum from this study into next week, next month, and next year? Use this lesson as a time to not only review what you discovered but also determine how you'll stay on track tomorrow.

Talk about your plans with small-group members, commit your plans to prayer, and then do what you say you'll do. As you move forward with a renewed sense of purpose, you'll become more confident facing the stresses you face every day. And with the confidence will come, gradually, more success at becoming the man you want to become.

READ I Can't Keep Up with the Workload

Job 30:27

> My stomach's in a constant churning, never settles down.
>   Each day confronts me with more suffering.

THINK

- What about your workload tends to churn away in you and keep you in low-level anxiety or distress?
- What role could your faith play in settling such anxiety, or at least reducing it?

PRAY

God, remove from me . . .

LIVE

- How does God's truth impact the "next step" in your journey?
- How will you get there?
- How will you be held accountable?

READ   I Don't Make Enough Money

Hebrews 13:5-6

Don't be obsessed with getting more material things. Be relaxed with what you have. Since God assured us, "I'll never let you down, never walk off and leave you," we can boldly quote,

> God is there, ready to help;
> I'm fearless no matter what.
> Who or what can get to me?

THINK

- In what ways do you need to relax "with what you have"?
- In what ways do you need to claim the boldness and fearlessness of God's help and change your situation where you can?

PRAY

Lord, direct me . . .

LIVE

- How does God's truth impact the "next step" in your journey?
- How will you get there?
- How will you be held accountable?

READ   I Can't Do Enough to Satisfy My Wife

1 Corinthians 7:17

Don't be wishing you were someplace else or with someone else. Where you are right now is God's place for you. Live and obey and love and believe right there. God, not your marital status, defines your life.

THINK

- Describe the occasions in your marriage when you wish "you were someplace else or with someone else."
- What would help make it possible to "live and obey and love and believe right there" with your wife without the stress of feeling you're not satisfying her?

PRAY

God, show me how . . .

LIVE

- How does God's truth impact the "next step" in your journey?
- How will you get there?
- How will you be held accountable?

READ My Kids Demand Too Much of Me

Psalm 143:7

> Hurry with your answer, GOD!
> > I'm nearly at the end of my rope.

THINK

- What do you desire most from God in relation to your kids?
- What things can you do (or ask others to help you with) that will reduce kid-related stresses?

PRAY

God, help me . . .

LIVE

- How does God's truth impact the "next step" in your journey?
- How will you get there?
- How will you be held accountable?

READ Who's Looking Out for Me?

Matthew 6:34

"Give your entire attention to what God is doing right now, and don't get worked up about what may or may not happen tomorrow. God will help you deal with whatever hard things come up when the time comes."

THINK

- What are one or two "tomorrow" things you wish you wouldn't get worked up about?
- How can you practice giving "your entire attention to what God is doing right now," particularly in relation to those "tomorrow" things?

PRAY

God, help me see you . . .

LIVE

- How does God's truth impact the "next step" in your journey?
- How will you get there?
- How will you be held accountable?

READ   I'm Not Holding Up My End of a Friendship

Proverbs 25:25

> Like a cool drink of water when you're worn out and weary
> is a letter from a long-lost friend.

THINK

- Name one friend who needs a "cool drink of water" from you right now.
- How might you take better care of this friendship?

PRAY

Lord, direct me . . .

LIVE

- How does God's truth impact the "next step" in your journey?
- How will you get there?
- How will you be held accountable?

READ My Leash Is Too Short

Matthew 11:29-30

"Learn the unforced rhythms of grace. I won't lay anything heavy or ill-fitting on you. Keep company with me and you'll learn to live freely and lightly."

THINK

- What is "heavy or ill-fitting on you" at the moment? What's restricting you from living freely and lightly?
- What's one thing you could do to keep company with Jesus in a new way?

PRAY

God, free me . . .

LIVE

- How does God's truth impact the "next step" in your journey?
- How will you get there?
- How will you be held accountable?

NOTES

LESSON 1

1. Interview with Carmen Renee Berry, "Coping with Stress and Burnout in Youth Ministry," *Youthworker* (Spring 1995), pp. 55-56.
2. Richard A. Swenson, M.D., *A Minute of Margin: Restoring Balance to Busy Lives* (Colorado Springs, Colo.: NavPress, 2003), reflection 15.
3. Tim Hindle, *Reducing Stress* (New York: DK Publishing, 1998), pp. 34-35.

LESSON 2

1. Thomas H. Holmes and Richard H. Rahe, "The Social Readjustment Rating Scale," *Journal of Psychosomatic Research* 11 (1967), pp. 213-218.
2. Mary Pipher, Ph.D., *The Shelter of Each Other: Rebuilding Our Families* (New York: Grosset/Putnam, 1996), pp. 77, 95. Used with permission of G.P. Putnam's Sons, a division of Penguin Group (USA), Inc.
3. Richard A. Swenson, M.D., *A Minute of Margin: Restoring Balance to Busy Lives* (Colorado Springs, Colo.: NavPress, 2003), reflection 162.

LESSON 3

1. Sherwood Anderson, *Perhaps Women* (Mamaroneck, N.Y.: Paul P. Appel, 1970), pp. 43-44.
2. Margaret Popper, "Lost Job, Lost Spouse," *Business Week* (12/17/01).
3. Bill Thrall, Bruce McNicol, and John Lynch, *TrueFaced: Trust God and Others with Who You Really Are* (Colorado Springs, Colo.: NavPress, 2003), p. 96.

LESSON 4

1. J. O. Berry and W. H. Jones, "The Parental Stress Scale: Initial Psychometric Evidence," *Journal of Social and Personal Relationships* 12 (1995), pp. 463-472.
2. John Marks, "Time Out," *U.S. News & World Report* (12/11/95), p. 86. Copyright 1995 U.S. News & World Report, L.P. Reprinted with permission.

3. Larry Crabb, *Inside Out* (Colorado Springs, Colo.: NavPress, 2003), p. 116.
4. Robert Bly, *Iron John: A Book About Men* (New York: Perseus Books, 1990), pp. 31, 41.

LESSON 5
1. Larry Crabb, *Inside Out* (Colorado Springs, Colo.: NavPress, 2003), pp. 145-146.

LESSON 6
1. Brennan Manning, *Abba's Child: The Cry of the Heart for Intimate Belonging* (Colorado Springs, Colo.: NavPress, 2002), pp. 128-129.
2. Hara Estroff Marano, "The Dangers of Loneliness," *Psyched for Success* (August 21, 2003).
3. Nancy Rosenberg, *Outwitting Stress: A Practical Guide to Conquering Stress Before You Crack* (Guilford, Conn.: Lyon's Press, 2003), pp. 32-33. Copyright © 2003 by Nancy H. Rosenberg. Reprinted by permission of The Lyons Press, a division of The Globe Pequot Press, Guilford, CT.

LESSON 7
1. L. John Mason, *Stress Passages: Surviving Life's Transitions Gracefully* (Berkeley, Calif.: Celestial Arts, 1988), p. 170.
2. Brian Chichester, et al., *Stress Blasters: Quick and Simple Steps to Take Control and Perform Under Pressure* (Emmaus, Pa.: Rodale Press, 1997), pp. 106, 131.
3. Brennan Manning, *Abba's Child: The Cry of the Heart for Intimate Belonging* (Colorado Springs, Colo.: NavPress, 2002), p. 120.